CAMBRIDGE
A Photographic Celebration

Fotogenix Publishing

Photography by Andrew Pearce

Text by Kim Wallis

This book is dedicated
to all those who work to preserve the beauty of Cambridge

Cloisters at Trinity College

First published in Great Britain 2004
by Fotogenix Publishing
01767 677086
www.fotogenix.co.uk

Photography: Andrew Pearce ARPS
Author: Kim Wallis
Design: Debi Pearce
'Welcome to Cambridge' © Barbara Moss (Page 93)

Printed in Great Britain by Butler and Tanner Ltd, Frome, Somerset

ISBN 0-9547355-0-1

Select photographs reproduced by kind permission of
the Masters, Principals, Presidents,Provosts, Fellows and Scholars of:
Peterhouse, Clare, Corpus Christi, Gonville and Caius, King's, Queens', Jesus, Christ's, St. John's,
Trinity, Trinity Hall, Emmanuel, Magdalene, Downing, Sidney Sussex and Pembroke Colleges.

Right: Senate House Passage

Previous page: The Cambridge Backs at dawn

CONTENTS

Right: King's College from the Backs
Overleaf: The River Cam by King's College

FOREWORD

At six o'clock each morning while the city slumbers I start work. In winter the streets are silent. King's College Chapel looms above me, a dark silhouette towering above the empty street.

In spring the birds are singing and ducks straying from the River Cam and the college ponds run past, chasing each other along the main roads. Once, one laid an egg in front of me on a nearby pub doorway, before walking nervously away. I left it for the publican.

In summer after the 'May Balls', held to celebrate the last exams, students struggle home at dawn in crumpled dinner jackets and party frocks. Some hold hands and seem to be walking on air, in love. Others laugh and joke. In what other town in the country would a roadsweeper collect so many discarded champagne bottles?

My favourite spot in the early morning is the bridge across the Cam in Garret Hostel Lane. How many other towns have a view like this of towering trees and grass and water, only five minutes walk from Marks and Spencer?

Allan Brigham has worked for Cambridge City Council for 25 years as a member of the Street Scene team who look after the streets and open spaces. He is a well-known local historian, East Anglian 'Blue Badge' Tour Guide, and Chairman of the Friends of Cambridge and County Folk Museum.

25 years ago I came to Cambridge for six months to see a friend and save some money. I never intended to stay and didn't understand how people could live in a town surrounded by flat ploughed fields with no hills nearby. Slowly, by accident, Cambridge became my home. I still haven't saved any money (and probably never will)! But now I can live without hills because here the countryside comes right into the city.

Parks, commons and gardens encircle the central area, while green corridors like Hobson's Conduit lead out of the city.

These, as much as the formal architecture, are what make Cambridge one of the most beautiful cities in Europe. Three million visitors a year come to Cambridge, to take home memories of the city which is my home. Andrew Pearce's wonderful photographs in this book illustrate perfectly the attractions that draw them here.

But Cambridge is not a museum. It is an exciting and prosperous city. Research projects begun in the University have coupled with local skills developed in the traditional instrument companies to create an internationally recognised centre for the technologies of the 21st century: 'Silicon Fen'.

All visitors should survey the city from the top of the Norman castle mound standing guard above the river crossing that gave the town its name. Cambridge seen from here is not very big. But it becomes bigger the further away that you are from it! In California and Hong Kong people have heard of Cambridge who know nothing of far larger cities like Birmingham or Cardiff. It is a small city with an international reputation. I am very lucky to live here. (And proud to help keep it beautiful).

Allan Brigham, March 2004

Left: Queens' Mathematical Bridge

9

SETTING THE SCENE

The origins of Cambridge are firmly entwined with its much-loved namesake, the peacefully meandering River Cam. Farmers had already settled along the Cam's quiet riverbanks three thousand years before the Romans marched north to re-organise the local tribes.

The Romans discovered the settlement's strategic potential while constructing roads between Colchester and Leicester. By 70AD they had constructed a ford across the river, where the first wooden 'Great Bridge' was later built. It was conveniently close to the only hill in the area, and here they built a fort, utilising the views to control the river crossing. With typical efficiency, the Romans developed a fenland canal system that increased river trade. Cambridge's City Arms still depict boats and seahorses, reflecting its early status as the most southerly port from the Norfolk coast.

Trade continued through the Dark Ages of Anglo-Saxon and Danish occupation. Cambridge had the economic advantage of its navigable river with sea routes to and from European markets. Furthermore, its site where trade routes intersected between fen and forest areas was ideal. In 1068 the Normans marked its importance by settling here, and constructing a motte and bailey castle on the site of the Roman fort.

Various religious orders settled too, and in 1209 their academic reputation attracted a few scholars fleeing from trouble in Oxford. These student groups and their masters, led by a chancellor, soon formed the University. The lively young scholars managed to find time between study and prayer to add mischievous colour to town life. The townsfolk, meanwhile, raised the price of food and lodging. To their mutual benefit, Peterhouse began a college system of supervising its scholars in 1284.

Not long after this, the Black Death raged through East Anglia, decimating the number of priests as well as the local population. Wealthy patrons responded to this shortage of clergy by endowing new colleges, thus beginning the trend for impressive halls of learning that greatly enhanced Cambridge's academic reputation, as well as its skyline.

Cambridge was granted city status in 1951 and it is still a centre of commercial excellence. Groundbreaking research by the University and companies in the science parks, has earned it the name 'Silicon Fen'. The University currently has 31 colleges, and bicycles reign supreme as over 15,000 students pedal the streets. On the mound where the castle once stood, panoramic views across Cambridge and its verdant open spaces instil a sense of the city's enduring beauty. Magdalene Bridge has long since replaced the original 'Great Bridge', but the river flows on.

Left: Castle Mound

400	The Romans departed
875	River crossing chronicled at site of Magdalene Bridge
1025	St. Bene't's Church built
1068	Normans settled and built castle
1130	Round Church built
1209	1st scholars arrived, escaping Oxford riots
1284	Peterhouse founded
1326	Clare College founded
1348	Gonville College founded as University Hall
1352	Corpus Christi founded
1441	King's founded
1448	Queens' founded
1496	Jesus College founded
1505	God's House refounded as Christ's College
1511	St. John's founded
1536	King's Chapel completed
1546	Trinity College founded
1584	Emmanuel College founded
1610	Hobson's Conduit built
1616	Cromwell studied at Sidney Sussex
1638	Clare Bridge built
1724	Pepys bequeathed his library to Magdalene
1749	Mathematical Bridge built
1800	Downing College founded
1829	1st Boat Race between Oxford & Cambridge
1837	Building of Fitzwilliam Museum began
1846	Botanic Garden established on Trumpington Road
1849	Great Fire of Cambridge
1855	Market established on present site
1866	1st May Ball
1875	Newnham College founded for women
1975	Trinity founded England's 1st science park, in Cambridge
1977	Robinson College, the most recent college, founded
1988	Magdalene 'capitulated' to admit women students

11

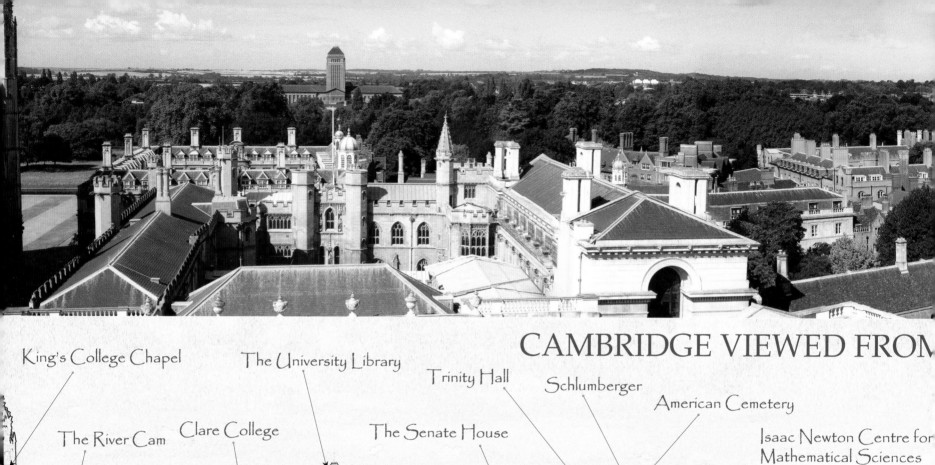

CAMBRIDGE VIEWED FROM

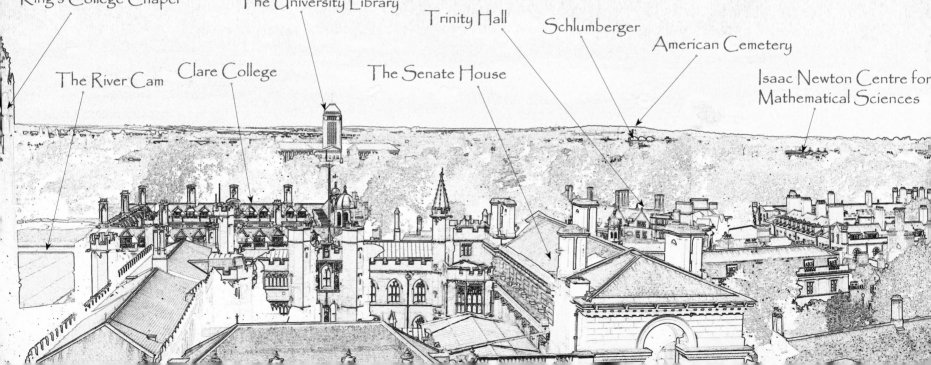

King's College Chapel

The University Library

Trinity Hall

Schlumberger

American Cemetery

The River Cam

Clare College

The Senate House

Isaac Newton Centre for Mathematical Sciences

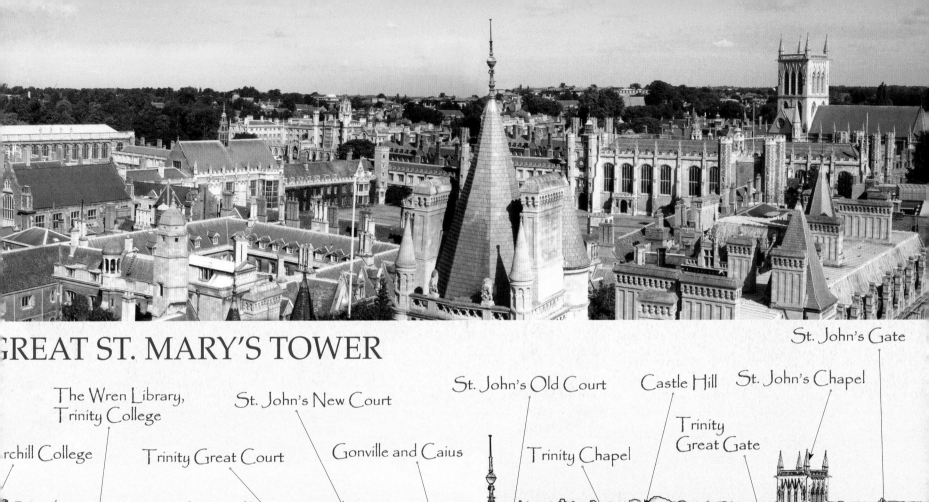

GREAT ST. MARY'S TOWER

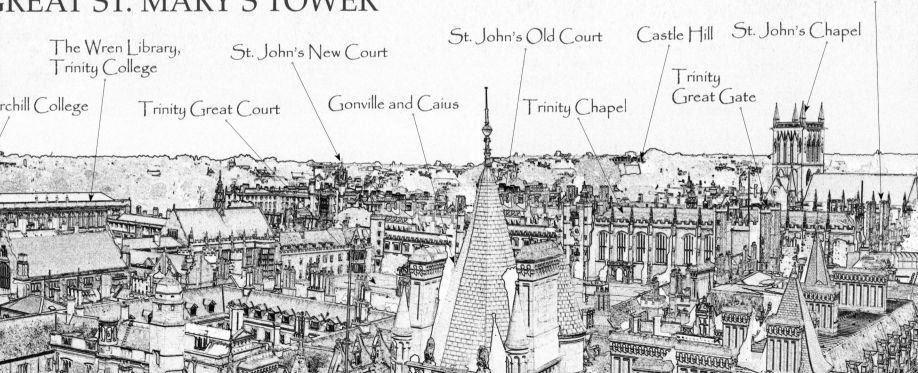

St. John's Gate

The Wren Library,
Trinity College

St. John's New Court

St. John's Old Court

Castle Hill

St. John's Chapel

rchill College

Trinity Great Court

Gonville and Caius

Trinity
Great Gate

Trinity Chapel

Pepys Building: Magdalene's buildings are built in brick; the neo-Classical front of the late 17th century Pepys building, constructed of Ketton stone, is the exception.

First Court: Fuchsias offset the austerity of First Court's monastic stonework.

MAGDALENE

Magdalene basks peacefully along a stretch of ancient river bank. Its length is divided neatly in two segments at the point where Magdalene Bridge, believed to be the city's oldest river crossing point, crosses the Cam. Records of the original 'Great Bridge' date back to around 875 AD.

Close by are Castle Hill's Roman garrison remains, and evidence of a paved causeway has been found in Magdalene's grounds. At the crossroads near the gatehouse, a bronze pillar marks the place where 14th century silver treasure was recently unearthed.

In 1428 the Abbot of Crowland chose this site north of the river, at some distance from the town to avoid temptation and noise, and founded a hostel for the student monks of local Benedictine orders. Patronised by the Dukes of Buckingham, it became Buckingham College.

After the dissolution of the monasteries, Thomas Audley refounded it as the College of St. Mary Magdalene in 1542. As King Henry VIII's Lord Chancellor, and his master's willing servant, Audley infamously presided over the trials of Sir Thomas More and Bishop Fisher. He apparently favoured rededicating the college as Magdalene, pronounced 'maudlyn', because it sounded like his name.

From Magdalene Street little can be seen of the beautifully kept gardens and lawns sloping gently riverward. First Court's old monastic buildings and chapel with its dark Victorian oak pews also lie hidden behind the east gate.

Riverside: College gardens fronting the river are a glorious mass of daffodils and delicate willow leaves in spring.

A visitor in 1710 scathingly described the few books in Magdalene's library as 'all ... entirely overgrown with mould'. He would have formed a very different opinion in 1724 when the college inherited 'for the benefit of posterity' a magnificent library of 3000 volumes, the entire collection of its illustrious scholar, prominent naval administrator Samuel Pepys. Magdalene also has Pepys' famous shorthand diaries of the 1660s in which he vividly observed people and life in London. Exquisitely bound, the rare manuscripts and books are arranged by size within their original oak bookcases in Second Court's intriguing asymmetrical Pepys Building. A fine portrait of Pepys is displayed in the college hall.

Early benefactors distinguished themselves by being executed or dying young and Magdalene was poor, despite its rich library. In the 20th century, finances were revitalised by the generosity of Old Members as well as the benevolence of a wealthy Master, the prolific author A.C. Benson, who wrote the words for *Land of Hope and Glory*.

In the 1950s when the college needed to expand, the only area available lay across Magdalene Street. Sympathetic conversion of an old brewery and a number of pretty 16th century cottages has produced the friendly open courts situated behind the west gate.

Facing page: The serenity of Magdalene's gardens in spring provides an invitation for rest and reflection.

Overleaf: Magdalene's early summer display of wisteria is complemented by fragrant stocks.

Magdalene's elegant hall, which is illuminated by candlelight alone

ST. JOHN'S

Drama and intrigue preceded the establishment of St. John's College upon the site of the impoverished Hospital of St. John. Its foundress was the devoted mother of King Henry VII, Lady Margaret Beaufort, a woman of noble character whose virtue and charity 'were the only crowns she affected to wear'.

Committed to the ideals of religious education, with the help of her adviser and confessor John Fisher, the devout Catholic Bishop of Rochester, she pledged shortly before her death to provide for the college. Unfortunately the memorandum concerning this was not included in her original will and therefore in doubt. The expense of establishing the new college was such that the other beneficiaries of the will furiously contested the provision. St. John's foundation charter was drawn up in 1511, but it was a full year before Bishop Fisher's respected testimony finally persuaded the Archbishop of Canterbury to prove the will.

The college inherited some land along with the hospital it replaced, but early on it suffered financially. Lady Margaret's will had specified that revenue upwards of £400 per annum should be used to establish the college, but in 1515 Henry VIII, as residual heir to her estate, claimed his inheritance. Fisher struggled to secure further funding, and both he and his friends generously endowed St. John's with money and land themselves. Bishop Fisher was later elected Chancellor of the University for life, but his sense of honour brought about his execution in 1535 alongside Sir Thomas More. This was the penalty for their loyalty to the Pope, in refusing to swear allegiance to King Henry VIII, who had declared himself supreme head of the Church.

The tower of St. John's Chapel

Finances had improved by the mid 1800s when Bursar William Bateson organised the ambitious replacement of the original hospital's 13th century chapel with a much larger square-towered French Gothic style version. A new Master's lodge and an extension to the hall were added at this time, partially funded by benevolent donations from the fellows.

Opposite: the cloisters of New Court

The college's reputation for upholding honour was again evident when it staunchly supported King Charles I during the Civil War. Cromwell punished the college cruelly. His soldiers plundered its treasures, used it as a prison and a number of fellows were expelled for their loyalty to the King.

St. John's is admired for its wonderful blending panoply of courts. Its first two Masters augmented college coffers with wise management, enabling the building of First Court. However, the contract to build the similarly impressive Second Court some 80 years later ruined its builders, one of whom landed in prison. 17th century Third Court, which houses the Old Library, is connected by the Bridge of Sighs to the fabulously opulent neo-Gothic New Court, affectionately known as the 'Wedding Cake' for the intricate detail of its central tower.

St. John's has received many royal visits, and one unusual caller too. In November 1777 an exhausted stag took refuge from hunters in staircase G of First Court, after a long cross-country chase.

Above: Although its beauty needs no adornment, in 1956 cheeky students added their own touch to the Gothic style Bridge of Sighs, built in 1831. They punted a Mini upriver and suspended it, wheels just above the water, from the bridge.

Left: Near the Scholars' Garden is 16th century Merton Hall. It is attached to the School of Pythagoras, which in 1231 was the only stone house in Cambridge and the home of the town's first recorded mayor, Hervey fitzEustace.

Opposite: The 'Wedding Cake'

The Backs, leading to the Wren Bridge

Also known as St. John's Old Bridge, the Wren Bridge was built over a century before the Bridge of Sighs. When Sir Christopher Wren first suggested this elegant bridge in 1697, he had in mind the present Bridge of Sighs' location, leading over the river from Third Court. It was constructed 15 years later based on Wren's original design, but on the site of a previous bridge, following a lane between St. John's and Trinity.

St. John's quiet atmosphere has nurtured careers such as those of philanthropist William Wilberforce who fought for the abolition of slavery, as well as the poet William Wordsworth.

In the mid 19th century, mathematics was still the college's main area of study. Changes came towards the end of the 1800s, when St. John's fellow G.D. Liveing set the trend towards science by pioneering Cambridge chemistry.

Since then, physicists Sir Edward Appleton, Sir John Cockcroft, Paul Dirac and Abdus Salam have honoured the college with Nobel Prizes. In 1980 Frederick Sanger became the first person ever to win two Nobel Prizes for Chemistry.

The early 1980s were significant for the history of St. John's when the college's all-male tradition succumbed to the gentle touch, and women were admitted as fellows and students. Recently St. John's elected its first woman president, Professor Jane Heal.

Opposite: The Wren Bridge, with the Bridge of Sighs glimpsed beyond.

Overleaf: The tranquillity of St. John's College at dawn.

The Gate Tower

TRINITY

Henry VIII believed in doing things on a grand scale, from decreasing the powers of Rome to changing his wives. He spiced up English history with formidable exploits and benefited Cambridge with the foundation of mighty Trinity College in 1546.

Like its neighbour St. John's College, Trinity came into being under uncertain circumstances. Greedy advisers encouraged King Henry to seize the lands and sizeable wealth of all the colleges, as he had already done with the monasteries.

The University survived this threat thanks to the support of a wise and influential woman in its history: Queen Katharine Parr, Henry's 'surviving' sixth wife. Using a clever report that stressed the limited funds with which the University was providing such worthwhile education, she persuaded the king not only to spare its existence, but also to found a magnificent royal Cambridge college that might outshine his late political rival Cardinal Wolsey's establishment of Christ Church at Oxford. The existing adjacent colleges, Michaelhouse and King's Hall, were amalgamated to form Trinity.

In the Great Court Run, athletic freshers race around the Great Court, trying to complete a full circuit against the clock's 24 noon chimes: with less than 43 seconds before the double chimes have completed, this is no mean feat.

Henry further endowed it generously with lands and funds appropriated from the monks, as well as his own donations, to ensure its power and eminence. He died only weeks after the college's formal inauguration. In a strange paradox, having spent most of his reign at enmity with the Church, his final act was a pious dedication of his creation to 'the Holy and Undivided Trinity'.

His daughter, Mary I, began building Trinity's chapel with stone from the dissolved Franciscan friary soon after his death. Fulfilment of Henry's architectural vision for a grand college was left to Trinity's Masters. The wealthy 8th Master, Dr. Thomas Nevile, met this challenge with single-minded fervour and great imagination. He removed ancient King's Hall buildings and repositioned King Edward III's Tower in line with the chapel to create two acres of lawn for Trinity's splendid Great Court. The largest court in Oxford or Cambridge, it is the scene of The Great Court Run. This is an annual Trinity tradition famously recorded in the film *Chariots of Fire* (filmed at Eton) and it takes place at noon on the day of the Matriculation Dinner.

Sunrise over the spires of Trinity Chapel

The exquisite Wren Library with its cloisters beneath, is Trinity's finest building. Commissioned by his friend, the college's Master Isaac Barrow, Sir Christopher Wren asked no fee for the design of his masterpiece. At its completion in 1695, one of the world's greatest scientists, Sir Isaac Newton, held a fellowship at Trinity. Newton's former rooms can be pinpointed by the apple tree planted beneath his window. This is said to be a descendant of the tree that dropped his apple of enlightenment on the mysteries of gravity.

The library holds many of Newton's own reference books and other rarities including the 8th century *Epistles of St. Paul*. Modern manuscripts by alumni such as philosopher Bertrand Russell and A.A. Milne, the author of *Winnie the Pooh*, are also kept here.

Nevile's additions to Trinity were prolific. At his own expense he built the sublime Nevile's Court with its classical style cloisters as well as the Dining Hall, which emulates London's Middle Temple and is still used for daily meals. The beautiful lantern adorning the roof of the hall is a reminder of earlier times when a large college room's source of heat was usually a centrally situated brazier, with an open lantern above providing an exit for smoke and fumes. Numerous such lanterns punctuate the city skyline in Cambridge, each one intricate, unique, and proclaiming its own particular college's praiseworthiness.

Right: The Wren Library

In keeping with Henry VIII's ambition, Trinity is Cambridge's largest college. Henry's statue, above the outside entrance of the Great Gate, was another gift from Nevile. In an effort to make their august Founder appear more approachable perhaps, students have conscientiously replaced Henry's sceptre with a chair leg. Trinity's students have also put to use Nevile's elaborate fountain that decorates Great Court. Lord Byron made it his business to bathe under its carved Jacobean canopy, amidst official consternation. He further increased his notoriety by keeping a tame bear whose purpose he claimed was 'to sit for a fellowship'.

Trinity rooms did not have baths until the mid 19th century, when an enterprising student brought his own. He demanded that his bedmaker, one of that institution of venerable women who look after college housekeeping, should fill it every day from Great Court's fountain. Other bedmakers joined her indignation vigorously. A supply of piped water to the various college staircases was provided just in time to avoid a general strike.

Trinity members have carried off no less than 31 Nobel Prizes to date. As most of these have been in physics, chemistry and medicine, it deserves its reputation for academic brilliance in the sciences. The college has also produced six Prime Ministers and covers a broad spectrum of achievement. Henry VIII might justly look on Trinity as his finest monument.

Right: Trinity Bridge

Overleaf: Trinity's Great Court

TRINITY HALL

A friendly college with a history of rowing prowess, Trinity Hall has produced poets and novelists such as Robert Herrick and J.B.Priestley. So many of its distinguished lawyers commuted to London, that around 1730 the college provided milestones sporting the Trinity Hall crest (shown above) on the London to Cambridge road.

Right: Trinity Hall's most charming building is its small two-storeyed Elizabethan brick library, that still contains books secured with chains. It has a mysterious door nestled between leaded Gothic windows high above the riotous herbaceous display. No magic was practised here, however. The door once led onto a wooden gallery, now dismantled, that connected the library to the Master's Lodge.

Opposite: Front Court

Overleaf: Built in 1998, Jerwood Library's aesthetics make it a welcome, and indeed the only, modern addition to the Backs' riverscape.

Trinity Hall is a tiny gem set between the river and neighbouring Trinity and Clare. Its miniature chapel, built in 1366, is the smallest in Cambridge, and its delightfully colourful gardens inspired novelist Henry James to describe it as 'the prettiest corner of the world'.

The Bishop of Norwich, William Bateman, founded Trinity Hall in 1350 with practical intentions. After the Black Death's depredations upon local clergy, he wished to provide 'a perpetual College of scholars in the Canon and Civil Law'. Bateman was an accomplished lawyer and envoy to the Pope. The college still has his gift of the unique French silver gilt Founder's Cup, stamped with the arms of Pope Innocent VI.

CLARE

As one approaches Clare, the Classical lines of the chapel with its ornate lantern are seen through elegant gates.

Clare is Cambridge's second oldest college. It was established in 1326 as University Hall by Richard de Badew, the University Chancellor.

In its early years it suffered from severe loss by fire and was poor. Fortunately, the college's future was secured by the generosity and personal interest of the three times widowed Lady Elizabeth of Clare, King Edward I's granddaughter. It was renamed Clare Hall in 1338.

Under Lady Elizabeth of Clare's new and enlightened specification it became the first Oxford or Cambridge foundation to provide for a Master and fellows as well as undergraduate scholars residing in one single community.

Around that time bubonic plague, 'the Black Death', killed a third of East Anglia's population and half its parish priests. Lady Elizabeth's statutes spoke clearly of her wish to promote religious education to replace these ill-fated victims 'taken away by the fangs of pestilence'.

One of Clare's most famous alumni was the Bishop of Worcester, Hugh Latimer. He was a radical Protestant preacher and as royal chaplain to King Henry VIII, Latimer advised and supported the king in the dissolution of the monasteries during the early 16th century. He paid the price for this in 1555 when Mary I, the devout Catholic 'Bloody Mary', had him burned at the stake in Oxford.

The college has numbered many bishops and three archbishops among its fellows, a tribute to Lady Elizabeth's foresight.

Clare viewed from the immaculate lawns of the Fellows' Garden.

The Fellows' Garden displays spectacular planting schemes.

Walking towards the river through delicately wrought 18th century iron gates, one reaches Clare Bridge, the oldest remaining college bridge. Its graceful lines are punctuated by fourteen stone balls, which are its hallmark. Thomas Grumbold constructed it in 1638, receiving just three shillings. Apparently he retaliated for this underpayment by creating one of the balls with a segment missing. The ball with the missing segment is the second on the right, as one approaches the gardens.

Sadly, another great fire destroyed Clare's ancient buildings in 1521 and extensive rebuilding was necessary. The 17th century range surrounding the Old Court is thought to owe its refined beauty to designs by the great English architect Inigo Jones.

College renewal paused during the Civil War when Cromwell requisitioned Clare's stone building materials to fortify the castle. Further construction, including the Fellows' Library, resumed later that century. Clare's fellows are privileged to enjoy the touch and smell of some of the country's oldest books, 'incunabula', as well as many wonderful medieval manuscripts.

A special feature of Clare is the Fellows' Garden whose seclusion, lying so close to the city centre, is a marvel. Its lawns are annual springtime host to student plays. The old trees and the garden's beautiful planting schemes give it the reputation as one of the finest fellows' gardens in the city.

Clare was the first college to extend beyond Queen's Road. In 1924 building began on Memorial Court opposite Clare's Backs. Its library was endowed by a former Clare history scholar, Paul Mellon. He was once heard to remark fondly that Clare had taught him the true meaning of the 'three R's': Rowing, Riding and Reading.

Overleaf: Clare Bridge, 1638

KING'S

There is no doubt that King's College Chapel is the ultimate landmark in a city blessed with many wonderful buildings. It soars in Gothic splendour above the Backs' tranquil riverscape, a dignified statement of nobility.

It is certainly 'a work of kings' by virtue of its history, as it owes its existence to the patronage of no less than five successive monarchs.

King Henry VI was inspired to create a royal college after helping Pembroke Hall as a favour to the Chancellor of the University. He laid the foundation stone of 'The King's College of Our Lady and St. Nicholas' in 1441 at the tender age of 19. He had also founded Eton College and wished to provide further education for its scholars. For over 400 years King's College admitted only Etonians.

Henry VI's ambitious but unfulfilled vision for King's College included a court south of the chapel, a gate-tower, hall, library, chambers and lecture rooms. If these had been completed in keeping with the chapel, undoubtedly 'the like College could scarce have been found again in any Christian land'. Despite his enthusiasm it took 90 years to build the chapel.

Cascading summer colour near King's Chapel.

Following page: King's Chapel and Bridge from the Backs.

Right: The Old Lodge

The Gibbs Building was constructed in 1724. Its foundation stone was said to be the partially cut stone that was left when Henry VI was captured.

Henry's chosen spot for the college was too small: he needed more space for his grand plans. He 'requested' the purchase of shops, houses, a church, and even tiny God's House College that lay within the area. Although this request was compulsory, it took him three years to clear the site.

Work eventually began on King's Chapel in 1446 with Henry's master mason Reginald Ely as architect. It came to an abrupt halt 15 years later when Henry was imprisoned and murdered during the War of the Roses. Hearing of his capture, men working on the chapel immediately downed tools, abandoning one partially cut stone.

Slowly, as funds permitted, the building continued with the support of Edward IV, Richard III and Henry VII. Henry VIII funded the stained glass windows and donated the fine wooden rood screen that supports the chapel's organ. The magnificent fan vaulted ceiling, for which the chapel is so famous, was also constructed at this time, over a period of only three years.

After the chapel's completion in 1536, the rest of King's land was given over to grazing until the early 18th century, when plans for the fellows' building, named the Gibbs Building after its designer James Gibbs, came to fruition. A century later

there followed William Wilkins' lavish but much needed improvements to the college's life - the gatehouse and stone screen, dining hall and library, along with what is now known as the Old Lodge.

Over the centuries, the chapel has maintained a calm and regal presence through good times and bad. Oliver Cromwell stabled horses in the chapel during his rule, and used it as a drill hall, yet the windows miraculously survived. During the Second World War, all but the West Window stained glass was removed and hidden elsewhere in Cambridge. For security, a rumour was put about that it had gone to a Welsh mine.

King's has the tradition of naming its punts after the wives of English kings.

Details of early college living tell of tutors' duties that included the use of the rod on recalcitrant students. King Henry VI, who wrote the first statutes, had specified firm rules to keep students sober-minded. Long hair was forbidden, as were beards, colourful attire and gambling. Yet King's gave its scholars and fellows a calm ritualised life of 'quiet, scholastic competence, most of them without duties, to the end of their days'.

One old fellow would shuffle out every evening, prod the worms in the big lawn with his stick while muttering to himself 'Ah, damn ye; ye haven't got me yet', and return inside, not to be seen until the same time next day.

This unthreatened way of life was courtesy of the college's august background. As a royal foundation, King's students were granted exemption from examinations, an elevated status which caused considerable friction with the rest of the University until the privilege was revoked in the mid 19th century. After that time, King's dedication to academic excellence has been unfailing, most especially in literature. It has fostered many great scholars such as the poet Rupert Brooke, novelist E.M. Forster as well as the renowned economist John Maynard Keynes.

Cows graze on Scholars' Piece today as they have done for centuries.

Choristers making their way to afternoon chapel.

Left: The Gatehouse on King's Parade.

King's was the first college to admit female students, recent evidence of its characteristic openness and tolerance of the right to freedom of thought. Students over the years have felt free to leave their mark on King's too. The Cambridge Nightclimbers, a group of students who attempt to reach all the most unfeasible heights of Cambridge's spire architecture, have climbed the east turrets of the chapel. There they suspended a washing line with a jaunty selection of underwear to announce their feat. Observers will now note white spokes pointing down from the corner turrets, to prevent any further display of laundry!

King's musical tradition, envisaged by its founder King Henry VI to include daily singing of services in the chapel, has been faithfully maintained over the years by its famous choir. The 'crocodile' of boy choristers in their trademark Eton hats and gowns is a familiar sight, as they trot along on their way to chapel.

Every Christmas Eve, King's 'Festival of Nine Lessons and Carols' takes place in the chapel. A young chorister begins the procession singing as a solo the first verse of 'Once in Royal David's City'. This has been broadcast internationally since 1928, allowing the whole world to partake in the beauty of King's crystal clear acoustics, and the true spirit of Christmas.

QUEENS'

The combined sundial and moondial (1642) in Old Court is a great rarity. Old Court was joined to riverside buildings by long cloistered walks in the late 1450s, creating Cloister Court.

Queens' and Corpus Christi now have the city's only two intact medieval monastic-style courts. In the mid 16th century Queens' was enlarged by absorbing land from the adjacent friary. The college has reused ancient stained glass roundels depicting the Carmelite friars in the Old Library.

A clue to Queens' history lies in the apostrophe at the end of its name, for five of the country's queens have graced it with their patronage. Following the late, much-loved Queen Mother, Elizabeth Bowes-Lyon, Queens' patroness is at present Her Majesty Queen Elizabeth II.

Andrew Doket, the rector of nearby St. Botolph's Church, founded tiny St. Bernard's College in 1446, when King Henry VI was beginning his work at King's. Henry's feisty 18 year-old wife, Margaret of Anjou, was inspired by his grand plans and by the previous example of the Countesses of Clare and Pembroke. She decided that 'His and Hers' colleges would be appropriate for Cambridge. In 1448, she petitioned her husband to refound and rename St. Bernard's as Queen's College, because 'in the whiche Uniursite is no college founded by eny Quene of England hidertoward'.

Andrew Doket then enthusiastically set about building stately Old Court and the red brick buildings, now part of the President's Lodge. Dated around 1460, the President's Lodge is Cambridge's oldest riverside building. It is Queens' distinction to have kept more medieval buildings than any other Cambridge college.

After Henry's overthrow, King Edward IV's beautiful Queen Elizabeth Woodville benefited the college with a third founding by giving it its first proper Statutes in 1475, and further endowments were forthcoming from King Richard III's wife, Anne Neville. Despite the commitment from these early queens, records showing the college's name restyled from Queen's to Queens' only appear in the early 19th century.

Right: Queens' 15th century Cloister Court

During Henry VII's reign, Queens' President John Fisher introduced to the college Erasmus, the foremost Greek scholar of his time. Erasmus did not think much of English beer, weather or creature comforts generally, but he did appreciate the ladies. 'The English girls are divinely pretty. Soft, pleasant, gentle, and charming ...They kiss you when you arrive ... when you go away, and when you return', he wrote.

Queens' is a pretty college itself, with a relaxed and friendly atmosphere. It has a strong theatrical tradition. One of its more recent alumni is the actor and playwright Stephen Fry. In June, Cloister Court is stage to an open air performance by the college's drama society *The Bats*.

Queens' story would be incomplete without reference to its much admired landmark, the Wooden or 'Mathematical' Bridge. It was designed in 1748 by William Etheridge, built the following year by James Essex, and has since been rebuilt twice, in 1866 and 1905.

The absence of bolt or screw in its first construction is a good yarn, and the legend of Sir Isaac Newton's involvement may also be laid to rest, as he died in 1727. Etheridge's design used a clever mathematical system of structural trussing, and the deceptively simple little bridge deserves its fame.

Left and overleaf: The Mathematical Bridge, 1749

Queens' College from the Backs

Cloister Court's timbers were found preserved beneath plaster during renovation in 1912.

THE RIVER

The banks of the River Cam exude a Zen calm, only moments away from the city's frenetic hum. Its steady waters are serene, hypnotic even. Cambridge's growth has accelerated through the centuries, but the river's message is of timeless existence, a continuous thread through the relentless pace of adaptation.

The Cam has its source at Ashwell Springs and meanders some 16 miles before reaching Cambridge. The river's ancient name was the Granta, believed to mean 'great' river. 500 years before the Romans arrived, a trading community had already settled close to where the city stands, and subsequent Roman, Saxon and Norman rulers all recognised the river's advantages.

Above: Magdalene Bridge stands where the first wooden 'Great Bridge' was built.

Right: The Cam's clear waters reflect Trinity College Bridge, built in 1764. Until the early 1900s though, river water was still murky with effluent. Queen Victoria once paused upon Trinity Bridge while visiting the college, and asked its Master Dr. Whewell: 'What are all those pieces of paper floating down the river?' His swift reply politely spared the Queen the unpleasant reality of Cambridge's plumbing: 'Those, ma'am, are notices that bathing is forbidden'.

Left: St. John's Bridge of Sighs, built in 1831.

In 1627 King's was the first college to replace their wooden bridge with a stone bridge. Almost 200 years later this structure was rebuilt upstream from its previous central position when King's Backs were restyled. From the gate on Queen's Road, a winding path alongside Scholars' Piece now leads down an avenue lined with trees. Just before the bridge, the glory of King's Chapel and Clare College is revealed in full view.

Clare College's elegant bridge, constructed in 1638 of Ketton stone, is now the oldest remaining structure across the river. It was the first bridge built to a Classical design and is a familiar landmark with its 14 stone balls. Students once shocked the occupants of a punt gliding beneath Clare's bridge by tipping a papier-mache replica of a ball over the edge of the bridge. Panic turned to relief as it floated off down the river.

The stretch of land between the river and Queen's Road is known as the Backs. For centuries cattle have grazed these fields, that are now mostly luxurious lawns, interspersed with beautiful landscaped gardens and graceful walks leading down to the river. In the 1400s, before it became a college, St. John's probably began this trend for cultivation when it bought land to establish a herb garden and fishponds.

Right and above: The seasonal moods of Clare Bridge.

There are nine bridges crossing the Cam in the short distance between Magdalene Bridge and Silver Street Bridge. This was a favourite spot for skating when the river froze in the harsh weather of earlier times. Before purpose built indoor ice rinks became the fashion, the fens nearby produced most of England's champion skaters. During one particularly arctic winter more than a century ago, intrepid skaters made the journey all the way to Ely on the frozen river, but since the 1970s warmer weather patterns have prevented this fun.

The exhilaration of crisp winter mornings skating on the frozen river, and summer days spent punting slowly along its quiet waters, are pleasures that may be shared by everyone if the weather gods permit. Leisure activities are a fairly recent development though, and the Cam's historical importance to its community is more prosaic than poetic.

Until the railway arrived in 1845, the Cam was the chief means of freight transport for the entire district. It facilitated economic expansion within the productive rural landscape, and Cambridge has for many centuries been the county's prosperous centre of trade. Long before the colleges were built, the east bank of the Cam was a mass of quays buzzing with activity, and the river's eastern channel was improved to allow boats easier reach of the market place. Modifications to the river's course also accommodated King's Mill and Bishop's Mill, built upriver in the 900s, close to where Silver Street Bridge stands today.

Around 1120, local dignitaries persuaded King Henry I to proclaim that within the county, boats should only be allowed to exchange cargo at 'my borough of Cantebruge'. The king added another bonus to this important favour by commanding that only at Cambridge could local carts be loaded, and tolls charged. Business boomed.

Below left: Silver Street Bridge was designed by Sir Edward Lutyens and built in 1958, the most recent of the bridges sited there since the 1300s.

Part of Darwin College, The Granary, top left, and neighbouring Newnham Grange were once home to Charles Darwin's grand-daughter Gwen. She recalled spending hours as a child watching the equine traffic from her window. Fierce little trade ponies and bell-jingling hansom cab horses trotted constantly over Silver Street Bridge, sending up white dust clouds in summer and stamping through sticky mud in the wet winters.

Below: From vertical to horizontal - a punt provides each man with his own level of relaxation.

River transport vitally supported the town's two fairs, granted by King John in 1211. Midsummer Fair still takes place on Midsummer Common on the 22nd June every year. Stourbridge Fair, noted for sales of wool, hops, leather, iron and cheese, brought international fame and prosperity to Cambridge for over 500 years. Daniel Defoe was so impressed when visiting in 1723, that he declared it the greatest fair in the world.

In the 1600s, drainage of the fens increased the build-up of silt in the river and made navigation difficult. Goods rose in price, and flat-bottomed barges called 'lighters' proved better suited for transport. The Cam continued to flood sporadically, but this had a beneficial side effect, as building development was hampered along the river's wide flood-plain, saving the open meadows for enjoyment by later generations.

Right: Newnham Mill, Mill Pond's surviving flourmill, ceased operating in 1910. Its original waterwheel remains inside the building.

Left: Leisure punting, not milling, is the river business of today. Swans live quite happily alongside the punts.

Below right: Ancient King's Mill and Bishop's Mill were pulled down in 1928, leaving a quieter and emptier land-scape. These mills were long an integral part of daily life in Cambridge. Wheat and corn were brought by barge or horse-drawn wagon, and pulleys levered the bags up into the mills through a trapdoor in a protruding gable. After rail transport arrived, river traffic halted, though until the early 1900s Mill Pond was often still so full of barges carrying oil cake cattle feed, corn and coal that it was possible to walk down from boat to boat to beyond Queens' Mathematical Bridge.

Overleaf: Coe Fen

PUNTING

What more relaxing way to while away a hot summer's afternoon than to indulge in a slow journey along the waters of the Cam? Both Oxford and Cambridge are blessed with rivers that accommodate this civilised activity, but in Cambridge pleasure-seekers 'punt' while those in their sister city 'paddle'.

The punt's use for transport dates from medieval times. It is flat underneath with no keel, and its stability is perfectly suited for shallower waters. Today punting takes place for leisure, and Cambridge's favourite pastime is enjoyed by sybarite and the active alike. Those of a daring nature can balance themselves carefully at the rear of the punt, propelling the boat forward with a long pole. Others, more inclined to recline, may abandon themselves to trailing their fingers through the cool water, their most arduous task being to pour the champagne.

The stretch of river around Cambridge is divided into three levels. The lower river, below Jesus Lock, is the domain of rowers. Punting takes place on the middle river which offers cultural vistas along the Backs, and also on the top section extending past open meadows to Grantchester. Punts may be hired from near Silver Street Bridge and Magdalene Bridge.

An officer known as the Pinder is in charge of river wildlife conservation as well as Cambridge's commons, such as Coe Fen, where cows graze peacefully. The river is home to elusive water voles, as well as pike, trout, carp and eels, and many birds.

Ducks and both black and white swans mingle with the punts, while moorhens prefer the side channels. The bright blue flash of a kingfisher skimming the water's surface might reward an early morning visit, and greater spotted woodpeckers have nested near Clare. In the early evening, owls may sometimes be heard hooting along the Backs.

71

It is reasonably straightforward to manoeuvre a punt, propelling it by leaning back upon the pole and then releasing it from the riverbed with a twist. However, novices are well advised to bring a change of clothes in case of falling overboard. A stranded punter, clinging tightly to a slowly descending pole while the punt moves steadily away from him, is no unfamiliar sight on the Cam.

The best way to avoid getting wet is to avail oneself of a student punt chauffeur, who comes with the added bonus of a comprehensive store of interesting information and anecdote on town and college history. A 45 minute tour along the Backs accompanied by one of these boatered experts will seem like as many seconds, while one listens to lively stories that mix fascinating facts with some rather entertaining fictions.

Faith in the credibility of one's guide may be sorely tested upon hearing how Jesus planted one of the huge trees along St. John's Backs when he came to Cambridge. But then again, Jesus College is not very far away...........

St. John's Chapel and lantern

The Bridge of Sighs

The Mathematical Bridge yields a favourite tall tale. Inquisitive students supposedly wished to discover the secrets of its brilliant design without nut, bolt, screw or pin. After they had taken it apart, they could not remember the correct sequence for putting it back together again and bolts then became necessary to rebuild it. In fact, bolts were used from the bridge's initial construction in 1749.

Another popular fiction is that Trinity beat St. John's in a race to finish building their tower clocks. As the loser, St. John's was obliged to cease completion of their clock when Trinity won, but Trinity's clock gracefully chimes twice, once for Trinity, followed by a gentler note for St. John's. Pure fable, but St. John's clock face does indeed lack a working mechanism, and Trinity's clock does have a double chime.

Student chauffeurs may also relate amusing anecdotes of their own colleges. One such story was recently recounted with great relish about Magdalene College, the last male bastion to admit women in 1988. During a debate prior to this major capitulation, one fellow allegedly declared he saw no need to admit women, as Magdalene already had the cream of Cambridge: rich, thick and full of clots!

ROWING

For the people of Cambridge and 'the other place', Oxford, there is only one boat race, and that is The Boat Race. Competitive spirit roars at full throttle as two 8-oared boats, one from each University, race along a punishing four and a half mile stretch of London's River Thames between Putney and Mortlake.

The world famous University boat race makes news headlines every year, when by tradition the previous year's loser challenges the winner to another race. This pattern began in 1829 when Charles Merivel, a student at Cambridge, sent his friend Charles Wordsworth at Oxford a challenge to race over two miles at Henley-upon-Thames. Henley folk were inspired by this to start their own great event, the Henley Royal Regatta.

Cambridge's first Boat Club was formed by St. John's, whose large heavy craft was no match for Trinity's sleeker, lighter model when they raced in 1826. This meeting gave rise the following year to the local races known as the Bumps.

Right: Christ's Boat House

Left: The Bumps in progress

Listening to good advice

The hotly contested 'Lents' and 'Mays' are local Cambridge Bumping races between the colleges, and the town's Bumps occur in summer. Enthusiastic supporters line the two miles from Baitsbite Lock to the Pike and Eel at Chesterton, cheering vigorously.

The four day long Bumps evolved because the Cam is too narrow for adjacent rowing. Divisions of 16 boats start each race a length and a half away from one another, and row furiously to 'bump' the boat in front. Boats swap starting positions daily, according to

their bumping success. Crews that bump each day keep their oars, inscribed with the crew's names, as trophies. The winners are called 'Head of the River' and may celebrate by burning an old boat at their Bump supper party.

Overleaf: Clare Bridge 77

ABOUT TOWN

The Cambridge University Press, established in 1584, is one of the oldest printers and publishers in the world. The site of its bookshop overlooking Senate House and Great St. Mary's has sold books continuously since 1581, making it the oldest bookshop in England. Tennyson, Kingsley and Priestley among others gave literary presentations here.

Vernon McElroy's bronze tactile model of Cambridge, in front of Great St. Mary's, was commissioned by Rotary and unveiled in 2002 to commemorate Queen Elizabeth II's Golden Jubilee.

Pockets of emerald beauty along the tranquil banks of the river offset Cambridge's architectural glory to perfection, while the city centre yields interesting lanes and quaint alleyways to explore.

Early prosperity came from the Roman settlement's military traffic and the thriving riverside trade. After William the Conqueror's invasion in 1066, his infamous sheriff Picot controlled Cambridge. Contemporary monks recorded him as 'a hungry lion, a ravening wolf, a filthy hog', but he was obeyed, because he kept a well-armed castle. Picot multiplied taxes eightfold, but the town's trade continued to thrive nonetheless.

Cambridge has fortunately retained many of its ancient churches. The oldest, St. Bene't's (St. Benedict's), was built before the Normans arrived and still maintains its Saxon chancel, nave and tower. It lies sheltered behind Corpus Christi, who used it as their college chapel for many years. The church of the Holy Sepulchre opposite St. John's is a rarity. It is one of only four round churches in England and was consecrated in 1107 at the time of the first crusade, making it probably the world's oldest crusading church.

A short walk away, Great St. Mary's trees provide a soft evergreen backdrop for the Market Square. The church has combined University and civic ceremonial duties with its spiritual role for around 800 years. Many religious leaders such as Cranmer, Latimer and Ridley have preached in Great St. Mary's. In early times the University Chest, a strongbox containing valuable manuscripts, charters and deeds, was entrusted to Great St. Mary's safekeeping. During the Peasants' Revolt of 1381, it was broken open and the contents were burned in the market.

In the early 1200s, King John recognised Cambridge's trading importance and granted it charters to manage its own affairs. The market then was home to various stalls with potters, spicers, saddlers, butchers, fishmongers and poulterers among others, set in an L-shape around a central group of buildings. It ran down Market Hill, around to Peas Hill. However, no hill has ever existed here - the word 'hill' is ancient Cambridge usage meaning an open space. Today, the number of bicycles attached to iron railings illustrates how many cyclists appreciate the city's fenland flatness.

Right: Great St. Mary's Church. Breathtaking views of Cambridge can be seen from the church tower. The quarter-hour chimes of the tower's clock are famous. They were invented by Rev. Jowett of Trinity Hall in 1793 and later copied worldwide, most notably as the 'Westminster Chimes' of Big Ben.

The market has thrived here for over 1000 years, but in 1849 the Great Fire of Cambridge destroyed the central cluster of houses, creating its present square shape. Stalls are now a colourful mixture of flowers, fruit and vegetables, books and clothing old and new, crafts and souvenirs as well as fresh fish and meat. Next to the market is Rose Crescent, formerly the yard of the Rose Inn. In the 1600s Samuel Pepys stayed there, and once 'lay very ill, by reason of some drunken scholars making a noise all night'. The inn's balcony where election speeches were made can still be seen, overlooking the Market Square.

Lloyds Bank building was formerly Foster's Bank. Its interior is lavishly decorated with tiled walls and ornate high ceilings.

Before rail travel, many travellers heading north stopped off in Cambridge at its busy coaching inns. One of these, the Eagle, now survives as a popular pub opposite St. Bene't's. The stables have become a secluded courtyard resplendent with floral hanging baskets. In the 1950s, the Eagle was a favourite haunt of Francis Crick and James Watson, who celebrated in the pub after discovering the structure of DNA. The RAF bar at the back is named after Second World War airmen who drank there and left a poignant reminder of their presence by signing their names and regiments on the ceiling in candle smoke.

Above: Cambridge Market, looking along Rose Crescent to St. John's tower.

Overleaf: Cambridge Market seen from Great St. Mary's.

Right: The Eagle, once a 17th century coaching inn.

Above: The University Arms Hotel overlooking Parker's Piece and Hobbs' Pavilion.

Parker's Piece, the expanse of open ground off Regent Street, is a great recreational asset to Cambridge. Trinity owned the marshy land, known as Middle Field, until 1613 when they exchanged it with the town for fields to extend the college's Backs. It remained boggy and uneven until 1831, when it was drained and levelled to enable 'playing the manly game of cricket'.

The space is enjoyed all year, and is a favourite spot for picnic lunches in warm weather. A lamp standard in the middle of the vast lawn has had the name 'Reality Checkpoint' written on it from time to time since the 1970s. This allegedly marks a boundary between the academic world of the University and real life.

Right: The Catholic Church of Our Lady and English Martyrs, built in 1890.

Facing Page: Peterhouse, with Great St. Mary's and the United Reformed Church beyond.

During summer, afternoon games of cricket proceed, as ever, at a leisurely pace. The less energetic can observe in comfort from Hobbs' Pavilion, named after Jack Hobbs, the early 20th century cricketer who developed his skills on Parker's Piece. Football games were also played in the mid 1800s, and some say that association football originated in Cambridge. The measurement for goal spacing is reputedly taken from the distance between the regularly spaced trees surrounding Parker's Piece.

The cheerful copper turrets of the University Arms Hotel enliven the skyline alongside Parker's Piece. This imposing building was Cambridge's first purpose built hotel, created to provide convenient accommodation for the affluent 'Railway Age' travellers when Eastern Counties Railway opened the station in 1845.

Christ's College

Christ's College

Emmanuel College

The Isaac Newton Centre for
Mathematical Sciences

Pembroke College

Trinity Hall

St. John's College

Pembroke College

Senate House, built in the 1730s

ACADEMIA

Nearly 800 years ago a group of students fled from hostilities in Oxford, to continue with their studies elsewhere. They settled in Cambridge with good reason, as the presence of a number of established monasteries had already made it a recognised seat of ecclesiastical learning. By 1226 an organisation, with a set course of study and headed by a Chancellor, had formed the nucleus of the University.

In the 13th century, studies were mainly theological, and students as young as 14 years old were assigned to a specific Master. This Master would be responsible for the social and academic lives of a small group of boys during their entire course of education. When they were not studying, the scholars were in church, leaving little time for other pursuits. The ancient curriculum at Cambridge followed a set pattern, much like that in Italy, France and also Oxford at that time.

After a preliminary grounding in Latin, the foundation *trivium* of grammar, logic and rhetoric was pursued for two years. This was followed by the *quadrivium*, a four year course in arithmetic, geometry, music and astronomy. Examinations took the form of oral disputations in which a student himself would propose questions, and then 'dispute' or argue his ideas with the senior staff. After impressing the teaching masters with sufficient knowledge, he qualified as a Master of Arts, and could begin teaching.

During the early years, scholars were housed with their teaching masters in various kinds of accommodation, mostly privately owned. This led to problems of cost and control, and gradually colleges were established to provide secure lodgings where the lively young men, capable of much mischief in the short time available to them, could be properly supervised. Each college was controlled by a Master and a number of fellows who provided the teaching and fatherly care of the college's scholars.

Cambridge students now may study a far wider range of subjects, but they are no less high spirited than their 13th century counterparts. Senate House, where graduation ceremonies known as the Congregations take place, is often the scene of lively exploits. Athletic students attempt 'Death's Leap', a jump across Senate House Passage, from Caius College to the Senate House roof. Apparently survival rates are good.

A University Constable

Modern scholars share more than enthusiasm and pranks with the ancients. They come to Cambridge in a state of exhilaration mixed with trepidation. Most are away from home for the first time and must adapt quickly to a demanding workload. In the process, lifelong friendships are formed. Nowadays lectures are taken within the University department of subject choice. However, in the Cambridge tradition, students still enrol with a chosen college, where they lodge and receive meals as well as tutorial supervision.

Graduate scholars and their families gather on the lawns outside Senate House.

Above: University Constable in ceremonial dress

Below: A University Marshall attends the Deputy Vice-Chancellor

After successful *tripos* examinations taken over three or four years of study, undergraduates are admitted to their degrees at one of the University's Congregations. The graduands assemble at their colleges in order of degree precedence, clad in gowns and hoods which vary in colour by degree and status. The royal colleges of King's, Trinity and St. John's begin the procession to the Senate House, and the other colleges follow by seniority of foundation date. Inside the Senate House, the officiating Praelector presents up to four graduands at a time to the Vice-Chancellor. They then kneel individually before him while he holds their hands and pronounces their admission in Latin. The long-awaited moment of transformation has arrived: the student is now a proud graduate.

A number of University offices are now purely ceremonial, but some still perform their ancient duties. Proctors continue to enforce discipline within the University, and are assisted in this demanding duty by their constables, nicknamed the 'Bulldogs'. Proctors are present at all the Congregations. Bedells were 'men of substance' who carried out business on behalf of the Chancellor. In later years they were always graduates of the University. Today they attend the Chancellor at ceremonies, carrying their impressive silver maces over their shoulders.

Welcome to Cambridge

Far from her family now, the fresher alights at the station,
taking a taxi. The town comes racing to meet her.

Cautiously calling through cloisters, at last
she stumbles on her staircase, stands at the door
of her room, neat and ready to receive her.

The din in the dining-hall's daunting;
bookshops bewilder the browser with bargains;
the lecture list's long as a novel;
but welcomes are warm, overwhelming.

Finally, phoning her folks, she tells them,
'Everything's fine!'

Barbara Moss

*Excitement and
congratulations:
graduates consult the
exam results boards
by Senate House to
see how friends have
fared, and celebrate the
culmination of their
hard work.*

Overleaf: Graduation gathering at Christ's College   93

CHRIST'S

Christ's College nestles discreetly in the heart of Cambridge, an oasis of unexpected serenity separated by no more than a stone wall from the world outside where busy shoppers' feet beat a constant tattoo up and down the pavements of St. Andrew's Street. Stepping through Great Gate's original 16th century oak doors into First Court's tranquillity, one might easily have crossed back into earlier and less frenetic times.

Great Gate's impressive coats of arms, heraldic badges and the statue in its central niche all celebrate Christ's foundress, the generous and pious Lady Margaret Beaufort. The carved daisies or 'marguerites' also appear in honour of her name.

In common with many other colleges, Christ's had an earlier establishment in 1439 as the small college of God's House. Its founder was a priest, William Byngham, who wished to furnish the country with better qualified grammar teachers. Within ten years of its construction, however, King Henry VI wished to clear the land occupied by God's House to initiate his expansive plans for King's. He compensated by permitting it to relocate to its current site, and endowing it, partly with funds from priories appropriated during his father's war with France. In 1448, with its new charter, Henry also permitted it to teach its scholars in other faculties as well as grammar, as a normal college foundation.

After her son King Henry VII acceded to the throne, Lady Margaret Beaufort began to dedicate her energies to charity. Inspired by the advice of her confessor, Bishop John Fisher, her first good work was to refound God's House as Christ's College in 1505 by royal charter. She later went on to endow St. John's College.

Under its new title, Christ's was enlarged to take a Master, 12 fellows and 47 scholars. Lady Margaret gave it a munificent 4000 acres of land, mostly in nearby counties, to provide income for this growth. While Bishop Fisher arranged the college's academic structure, Lady Margaret's motherly influence was felt in her provision that the scholars should benefit from proper nursing if they were ill, and her stipulation that only two scholars, instead of four, should share a room.

Painted carvings of animals adorn archways and doors in and between the courts. These heraldic creatures, such as the Beaufort family's mythical antelope-like yales above the family's motto 'Souvent me souvient', (I remember often), all refer to the foundress Lady Margaret and her son, Henry VII.

Christ's College benefits from a team of devoted gardening staff. Thanks to their efforts and expert planning, First Court's flower beds and windows have a seemingly endless year-round variety of colour, such as the display of plumbago detailed above and opposite.

Opposite: The summer glory of First Court

After its strongly Catholic beginning, from Elizabeth I's reign onwards the college maintained a religious tone of unfanatical but 'separatist' Puritanism. This philosophical approach is still typical of Christ's ethos and it has nurtured the careers of many great men with similarly open minds.

Field Marshal Jan Smuts, twice Prime Minister of South Africa and influential in founding the United Nation's forerunner, the League of Nations, was a student at Christ's who demonstrated this balanced outlook during his role as statesman within his country. Smuts planned South Africa's future to include active political involvement by native Africans, but such a liberal approach led to his defeat by the right-wing Nationalist Party at the 1948 elections. He was elected Chancellor of Cambridge University following this, a post he held until his death.

Charles Darwin, 'father of evolutionary biology', is renowned for the conclusions to which his rational thinking led him. Darwin was admitted to Christ's to study religion in preparation for life as a man of the cloth. His early student days were busy mostly in the pursuit of field sports. He developed a consuming passion for collecting beetles, which inspired his career in natural history and later led to his theory of natural selection. This twist of fate caused him to throw the Church, his original vocation, into a storm of outrage and controversy when he published his seminal work *On the Origin of Species* in 1859, after six years as a naturalist travelling around South America aboard HMS Beagle.

John Milton, 'a poet second only to Shakespeare', was another famous student. He was born in 1608, the year that King James I ordered the planting of 300 mulberry trees at Christ's to support the silk trade. One of these, called 'Milton's Mulberry', survives today. Milton supposedly liked to compose poetry beneath this tree.

Left: The 18th century Fellows' Bathing Pool with its summerhouse is thought to be the country's oldest private pool. Fresh water feeding the pool comes from Hobson's Conduit.

Overleaf: Early spring in the Fellows' Garden: perhaps the wonderful contrast between naked trees circled by carpets of delicate snowdrops and aconites will inspire another poet such as Milton, within Christ's secret garden.

Thomas Hobson, one of Cambridge's wealthiest citizens, made his fortune hiring out horses and transporting passengers and goods. He was also disposed towards charitable good works. However, Milton wrote of a huge banquet given by Hobson where the guests' gastronomic expectations were not charitably met: 'The guests, expecting a great cheare, they were all disappoynted: for what found they, thinke you? Nothing on my word, but each one cup of wine and a manchet of bread on a trencher, and some five hundred candles lighted about the room, which was a very light banquet, both for the inner man and for the eye'.

Opposite: Christ's Fellows' Garden rivals that of Clare College for beauty. It is approached through the classic Renaissance Fellows' Building, which is considered Cambridge's most important mid 17th century structure. This elegant building provides a backdrop for the colourful, imaginatively laid out herbaceous borders and ancient trees in the garden beyond.

Milton's Mulberry

EMMANUEL

Emmanuel's name, meaning 'God with us', proclaimed Sir Walter Mildmay's intention when he founded the college. A devout Puritan who had long been committed to education, he wished to produce priests of sober faith who would encourage godliness in ordinary people with straightforward preaching.

In this sentiment he echoed the aims of the Dominicans or Black 'Preaching' Friars whose early 13th century friary, complete with orchards, gardens, barns and fishponds etc he purchased for the establishment of Emmanuel in 1584. The similarity between the two institutions ended there, however. Efforts were made to eradicate traces of the site's Catholic origins. The plain new chapel was built north to south, in contradiction of traditional east to west alignment.

Emmanuel's beliefs remained steadfast, despite the persecution of Puritans that pre-empted the Civil War. A third of the Cambridge number who sailed for the Americas to escape these Laudian reforms were Emmanuel men. Among them was a young graduate named John Harvard, who bequeathed funds and his library to found a new school that later became Harvard, America's first University.

Left: Front Court, viewed from the Wren Chapel cloisters

Emmanuel has a number of gardens, some private, some open. One of the latter is Chapman's Garden, named after one of its fellows, who had sole use of it until his death in 1913. Its peaceful pool is surrounded by a specimen Chinese 'fossil' tree and two tulip trees that bear large tulip-shaped flowers in June.

The Fellows' Garden is dominated by the languid weeping branches of a magnificent 200 year old Oriental plane tree.

Wendy Taylor's 1994 sculpture 'The Jester' invigorates Emmanuel's Paddock gardens.

Thomas Young is said to have arrived at his famous wave-theory of light after watching the rippling patterns made by birds swimming on Paddock's pond. Once the Dominicans' fishpond, and fed by Hobson's Conduit, it is now home to a colourful variety of ducks. Friendly porters have a supply of duck food for visiting children to feed these privileged birds.

During the Civil War Emmanuel fared well because of its Puritan zeal, as nearly all of its fellows supported Cromwell's regime. Many of them filled positions, left empty by deposed Royalists, as masters of other colleges. William Sancroft was one exception who supported the King; he became the college Master during the Restoration. He celebrated England's return to Higher Anglicanism in the late 1660s by commissioning Sir Christopher Wren to design a new chapel which replaced the earlier barn-like Puritan structure. Constructed of pink-flushed Ketton stone, this Baroque chapel is Emmanuel's finest building. It is realigned east to west, and flanked by round-arched loggias with a long gallery 'for exercise in bad weather'.

Emmanuel has always valued individualism in its scholars. In the mid 18th century, Emmanuel students displayed a strong independent streak. The story goes that a man's corpse mysteriously disappeared from Ditton churchyard (for use in the School of Anatomy), and was thought to be hidden within the college grounds. A stoic band of Emmanuel students refused to allow admission to both townsmen and highly placed University personnel. These dedicated scholars continued to fight off their superiors even after entrance had been gained by breaking down the college wall. After the Town Clerk had cleared the mob by reading the Riot Act, the corpse was discovered the next morning floating in a college pond.

Opposite: The Queen's building, opened in 1995, behind Emmanuel's tranquil gardens.

Overleaf: Paddock's pond.

DOWNING

Hidden behind an unassuming gate off Regent Street lies Downing College, whose elegance is a rather special visual treat, particularly in springtime.

Downing was Cambridge's first college to be established without connection to any religious institution. It was founded over 50 years after the death of its benefactor Sir George Downing, due to lengthy legal disputes that depleted the funds he bequeathed for the college's establishment. Sir George would not have approved, as the Downing family, who once owned the land upon which No.10 Downing Street was built, were known for their thrift.

In 1807 building began, admirably creating the spacious atmosphere of 'an academic grove à la Aristotle' that its designer, William Wilkins, wished to achieve. Wilkins was full of enthusiasm for the project after an extended tour studying Classical architecture in Italy and Greece. Often compared to the style of an American campus, Downing is believed to be the world's first campus, for as Hugh Casson has pointed out, 'nothing like this existed in America at the time'. In the late 19th century, the college sold part of its 8-acre grounds; this became the Downing Site, now home to many of the University's laboratories and fine museums.

Above: Downing's pillars are a key element in Wilkins' neo-Classical design.

Opposite: Glorious mauve, yellow and white crocus stripe the vast lawns in spring.

JESUS

Near Midsummer Common, the 'country in the town' location of Jesus contrasts with the more open and heavily frequented colleges along the Backs, being accessible, luxuriously spacious and yet extremely private.

The college's impressive gate tower offers an awe-inspiring welcome as one approaches Jesus from a narrow walled alley known as 'The Chimney'. The cockerel rebus prominently featured on the tower is a pun on the name of the Bishop of Ely, John Alcock, who converted the existing buildings to an early Tudor style when he established the college. However, Jesus' monastic look reflects its 12th century origin as St. Radegund's Priory of Benedictine nuns.

Right: Danny Lane's glass sculpture. Jesus has a well deserved reputation for supporting the creative arts. A recent Master of Jesus, the erudite archaeologist Lord Colin Renfrew, began the acquirement of contemporary artworks. The college hosts regular sculpture exhibitions in The Close.

Left: Second Court's Waterhouse Building, built 1869-70.

When only two nuns remained at the nunnery, Alcock applied for its dissolution, declaring the nuns unfit 'by negligence...and dissolute disposition...occasioned by the vicinity of the University'. He himself was zealously ambitious to promote higher learning in the very University he claimed had corrupted them. In 1496 he founded 'The College of the Blessed Virgin Mary, St. John the Evangelist and the glorious Virgin St. Radegund', but fortunately the simpler name of the Jesus altar within the nuns' chapel has prevailed.

Dating from 1140, the chapel is Cambridge's oldest college building. It now includes a ceiling by William Morris and stained glass windows designed by Sir Edward Burne-Jones. Within the serene intimacy of adjacent Cloister Court's early English arches, there still breathe the reflective contemplation and prayer of nuns buried nearby. Not surprisingly, history is a college strength.

Many scholars of note have enjoyed Jesus' park-like gardens. The martyr Thomas Cranmer, first Protestant Archbishop of Canterbury, and compiler of the Book of Common Prayer, was a fellow here. Coleridge, the brilliant but wayward poet, ran away from huge debts at the college and joined the army under a pseudonym, only to be discharged four months later, as he kept falling off his horse.

In spring, spacious lawns provide the students with a vista of bright crocus colour.

Cloister Court

SIDNEY SUSSEX

Wise, generous investment by the gentle sex has established one third of Cambridge's ancient colleges. Sidney Sussex, small and intimate, is one of them.

Modest from the start, it was founded in 1596 by the legacy of the childless Lady Frances Sidney, widowed Countess of Sussex, who wished to create a 'godlie moniment for the mainteynance of good learninge'. The college statutes, based on Emmanuel's, zealously demanded a Puritan rejection of 'popery and other heresies'.

Oliver Cromwell entered the college in 1616. He left after a year, having acquired more skill in football than in Latin, according to a contemporary. After the Restoration a judgement on the Lord Protector's career was added to Sidney's Admissions Register: 'This was that great impostor, that most accursed butcher, who when the most pious King Charles I had been disposed of by foul murder, usurped the throne itself, and for the space of almost five years, under the name of Protector, tormented the three kingdoms with unrestrained tyranny'.

Many years earlier in 1224, during the life of St. Francis, friars of his order arrived in England. The Franciscans (or Grey Friars) soon came to Cambridge, where, after sharing premises with the town gaol for a time, they were given the future college site. Until their dissolution in 1538 they made an important contribution to the study of theology in the University. One of them, the philosopher Duns Scotus, is commemorated by a plaque in Cloister Court. Henry VIII gave the site to Trinity, and nearly all the Grey Friars' buildings were destroyed to provide stones for its chapel and Great Court. Trinity dragged its heels in selling the friars' land that had been chosen for Sidney Sussex. Although Queen Elizabeth I abstained from establishing colleges herself, she gave crucial support to Lady Frances' executors by sending a stern letter that persuaded Trinity to jump to it.

Later generations were more forgiving. Cromwell's head, severed from his embalmed body when he was hanged posthumously at Tyburn in 1661, was returned to Sidney Sussex 300 years after his death. It was quietly laid to rest in the ante chapel in 1960, close to window panels set with stained glass fragments that were once part of the Grey Friars' church windows, thereby reconciling Sidney's dual Puritan and Catholic origins.

Dedication and diligence from its earliest masters and fellows gave this small theological foundation a sound start in life. Later Sidney began to exhibit strengths in mathematics and science, and was one of the first colleges in Cambridge to build its own laboratory.

Overleaf: Ancient wisteria graces Hall Court in summer.

Sidney's gardens are described as 'the sweetest lovers' walk in Cambridge'.

GONVILLE AND CAIUS

Approaching Gonville and Caius through the Gate of Humility, a unique avenue of Swedish Whitebeam trees within Tree Court welcomes one to the homely charm that is the college's essence.

A Norfolk rector, Edmund de Gonville, established Gonville Hall in 1348-9 during England's worst outbreak of bubonic plague, the Black Death. He died three years later and his friend Bishop Bateman of Norwich set out its course of study in law, medicine and theology. The Bishop completed its foundation by moving it next door to his own project, Trinity Hall. Enjoying superb views down King's Parade, the quiet sheltered courts belie its prime central location.

Poverty beset Gonville Hall for 200 years until its second founder, another Norwich man and a fellow of the college, John Keys rescued it. Keys took the Renaissance style Latinised form of his name *Caius* after postgraduate studies in Padua, and he grew rich doctoring wealthy London patients. In 1557-58, he secured the college's proper foundation charter and generously endowed it with his wealth. It became Gonville and Caius College, or Caius for short, and in 1559 he himself returned as Master. Dr. Caius was a character of many contradictions: conservative and dictatorial, yet displaying an avant-garde religious tolerance almost unknown in the 16th century. He was a great classical scholar as well as a talented doctor who started practical anatomy studies in England. The college maintains a strong medical tradition today.

Snowdrops in the shelter of Tree Court, with Senate House glimpsed beyond.

Dr. Caius kept immaculate records of students and their backgrounds and the college can prove an egalitarian intake from early on. Caius has accumulated some 11 Nobel Prizes so far, and produced outstanding scholars across a wide range of subjects.

In medicine, William Harvey first described how blood circulates through the body. Caius nurtured the talents of architect William Wilkins, whose prolific work can be seen across Cambridge from King's exquisite neo-Gothic gatehouse screen to the classic lines of Downing. John Venn's diagram occupies a place in every child's mathematical education, James Chadwick discovered the neutron and Francis Crick deciphered the code of DNA structure. Today, brilliant theoretical physicist, Caius fellow Stephen Hawking is Cambridge's Lucasian Professor of Mathematics.

Many Caius students have travelled far. Edward Wilson took the college flag to the Antarctic with Captain Scott, where they both died, and Thomas Manning was the first Englishman in Lhasa. Apparently Manning and the Dalai Lama played a game of chess, but we do not know who won.

One night, energetic Caius engineering students pursued 'the advancement of human understanding' by parking an Austin Seven van on the Senate House roof. The Civil Defence Force could not match this marvel of strategic planning in removing the van: it had to be dismantled by oxy-acetylene cutters.

Indulging in his taste for the symbolic, Dr. Caius built the college's three gates, which remain as a fitting monument to him. Students enter Caius through the Gate of Humility and they pass constantly under the Gate of Virtue while studying to attain wisdom. When successful, they leave through the marvellously ornate Gate of Honour, built in the 1560s, which features six sundials on its turret.

PEMBROKE

Pembroke follows in the footsteps of its sister college Clare as the third oldest in the city, and they share much in common. On Christmas Eve 1347, approximately ten years after Clare's revival by Lady Elizabeth of Clare, Edward III granted his dear cousin Marie de St. Pol, Countess of Pembroke, the licence to found The Hall of Valence Marie, as Pembroke was first called.

Like her close friend Lady Elizabeth of Clare, the Countess of Pembroke was a devout Catholic widow. She may well have followed her friend's example at Clare College in providing for one cohesive unit of Master, fellows and scholars whose focus was religious learning. With worship a priority, Lady Pembroke obtained a Papal Licence for her college to have its own chapel on site, thus making Pembroke the first Cambridge college to enjoy this privilege.

In parallel with Clare again, Pembroke has respected its foundress' aims by producing fellows of religious distinction over the centuries. One of these was the gifted linguist Lancelot Andrewes, Master of Pembroke and later Bishop of Ely, who took part in translating the King James Authorised Version of the Bible.

Pembroke also had its share of Protestant martyrs during the 16th century Reformation. John Rogers, John Bradford and Nicholas Ridley were all burned by Mary Tudor for their beliefs. Ridley joined Pembroke as a scholar in 1518. Destined to be Bishop of Rochester, as well as the college's Master from 1540-53, Ridley's affection for his college is commemorated by the path near the bowling green, named Ridley's Walk.

Left: The path leading from Old Court into Ivy Court.

Today's undergraduates walk in the same court and garden that was once home to Nicholas Ridley. Awaiting his death at Oxford in 1555, Ridley wrote a final fond message of farewell to Pembroke Hall 'of which study... yet the sweet smell thereof I trust I shall carry with me into Heaven'.

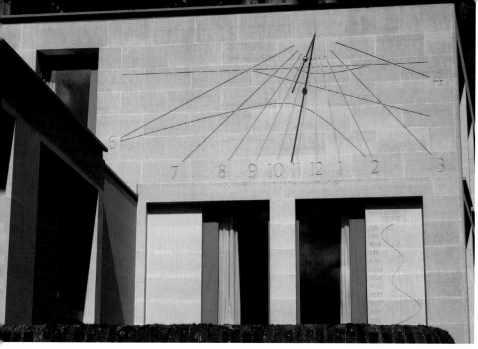

Sundial on Foundress Court, seen from Tennis Court Road

Pembroke's ancient entrance dates from its inception. The oldest such gateway surviving in Cambridge, its dignified welcome introduces a series of open courts and quiet, lovely gardens. The college's varying architecture reflects its progress over the years. New Court's 19th century flamboyance provides contrast to both Old Court's solemnity and Orchard Building's 1957 neo-Georgian simplicity, which fronts what is thought to be one of Europe's oldest bowling greens in use. The stunning elegance of Pembroke's latest stone addition, Foundress Court, built to honour its 650th anniversary, completes this display of the college's structural diversity.

During the Civil War, Pembroke supported the King by donating all its silver apart from the Foundress's Cup and the Anathema Cup (which places a curse upon anyone who removes it: 'let him be anathema'). Matthew Wren, another Pembroke Bishop of Ely and fervent Royalist, celebrated his survival of imprisonment by Cromwell by commissioning a new chapel for Pembroke. The enchanting Baroque chapel designed by his nephew, Christopher Wren, was Wren's first completed building when it was consecrated in 1665. The original chapel then became a library and today it is a meeting room.

Right: The reflective calm of Pembroke's dining hall

14th century Old Court

During the Elizabethan period, Pembroke began its long tradition of poets with the admission of Edmund Spenser. Ted Hughes, a recent Poet Laureate, has continued the line. Politics have also featured strongly. William Pitt distinguished Pembroke by becoming Britain's youngest Prime Minister at the age of 24, and it was at Pembroke that Ghandi stayed when visiting Cambridge in the 1930s.

The sciences have not been neglected in achieving academic balance within the college. George Gabriel Stokes, theoretical physicist and Master of the college at the time of his death, was elected Lucasian Professor of Mathematics in 1849. This century Pembroke has seen its geneticist Sir John Sulston sharing the Nobel Prize for Medicine for research on the human genome.

Pembroke suffered tragically during the Great War. It lost more than a quarter of all its men who served, twice the national average. The liberal atmosphere that has contributed to Pembroke's friendly and stable community is nowhere more clearly illustrated than on its War Memorial in a cloister adjacent to the Wren Chapel. All who fell are commemorated equally, with no distinction accorded to rank.

CORPUS CHRISTI

Uniquely among the colleges of Oxford and Cambridge, Corpus Christi was founded by ordinary townspeople.

In 1352 they bridged the gap between town and gown by sponsoring the University education of more priests after the plague. During the Civil War, Corpus showed similar community spirit by saving the college silver from both Cromwell and the King by sharing it out among its fellows and allowing them 'general leave of absence'. Despite its beginnings, it suffered from fire and looting in the Peasants' Revolt of 1381. This was angry protest against the 'candle rent' tax which the college levied upon the many houses it owned.

Archbishop Matthew Parker, Master of Corpus during the 16th century and its greatest benefactor, endowed the college with a large number of rare and valuable manuscripts preserved from the dissolved monasteries. To safeguard these, he instructed that no fellow should visit the library alone. Furthermore, 'If more than 25 volumes are missing at the end of the year the whole gift goes to Caius College, and if they are similarly careless...on to Trinity Hall'.

Opposite: New Court, built in 1823. Its designer William Wilkins is buried in the chapel.

Overleaf: Old Court, built around 1370, was the city's first complete quadrangle court. It is now the oldest medieval example surviving in Cambridge. A plaque here commemorates Elizabethan dramatists Christopher Marlowe and John Fletcher who studied at Corpus at a time when scholars were severely beaten if they were caught speaking English instead of Latin.

Below: Scholars' chambers, as in Old Court, were organised going up named staircases rather than running horizontally along corridors.

PETERHOUSE

Peterhouse is the oldest college in Cambridge and marked its 600th anniversary in 1884. In celebration of this, fellow and famous scientist Lord Kelvin arranged for it to become the first college with electric lighting.

Peterhouse is tucked cosily between the demure beauty of Little St. Mary's Church and the grandeur of the Fitzwilliam Museum on Trumpington Street.

Hugh de Balsham, Bishop of Ely, tried to accommodate those studying to be secular clerks within the Hospital of St. John, a religious house for the ailing poor. This failed when the brethren and scholars did not get on. In 1284 Bishop Balsham endowed the displaced scholars and their Master with two houses, and in 1287 bequeathed a large sum of money to support them while they studied. Peterhouse later acquired adjoining land to the south from a dwindling order, the austere Friars of the Penance of Jesus.

A high wall was built to enclose this land. It held a doorway onto Coe Fen for use by the Bishop who would visit by river and alight there. The doorway is still visible, although it has now been blocked up. A herd of deer once lived peacefully in this enclosure. They died out in the 1930s, but in the Deer Park and the nearby Fellows' Garden, a golden carpet of daffodils returns each spring to dazzle visitors.

Peterhouse's late 16th century library was sponsored by money and books bequeathed by its Master Andrew Perne, who was Vice-Chancellor five times. Dr. Perne, the only University high official to keep his post during Reformation changes, varied his allegiances with the times from Protestant to Catholic and then to Puritan. His cynical peers termed a new Latin verb *pernare*, which meant *to change often.*

The 18th century Fellows' Building facing the chapel in Main Court

The college's small, richly gilded neo-Gothic chapel with its magnificent stained glass east window was built in 1628 under the Laudian Mastership of Matthew Wren, Sir Christopher Wren's uncle. During the Civil War, the infamous William Dowsing, despoiler of so much beautiful religious decoration, displayed perverse glee in finding (and removing) 'so much Popery in so small a chapel'.

Poet Thomas Gray was a nervous 18th century 'Petrean'. He was anxious about fire, and made an escape route by fixing iron railings outside his top floor window looking down on Little St. Mary's. Students played a cruel joke on him one night by feigning fire, hoping to laugh at him as he shinned down a rope in his nightgown. The unfortunate Gray decamped across the road to Pembroke, to live a quieter life there.

Charles Babbage, initiator of a prototype computer, studied at Peterhouse. Other eminent Petreans include film star James Mason, politician Michael Portillo and the band Radiohead's Colin Greenwood.

Peterhouse has certainly mellowed since the time of its first rather strict statutes. Today it remains small and informal, secure in its prestige as Cambridge's oldest college.

Overleaf: Spring in the Deer Park.

CORNERS OF CAMBRIDGE

Cambridge's intriguing passageways and beautiful architecture yield an enchanting atmosphere, while eloquently describing a background of constant change. 'Adapt and survive' has been a key motif in the city's ongoing economic and academic success through the centuries.

Many buildings have experienced repeated alteration of use since their first construction, and survive because they have adjusted so well to the needs of the time. The Haunted Bookshop, down the tiny paved side street of St. Edward's Passage, operated as a drinking den during the 1800s, while on Market Square, Marks and Spencer's food hall was formerly the town centre cinema. Parts of the market and the Kite area have been restored from previous service as car parks.

Centuries of chimney smoke left the city with a grimy legacy, and conservation of its rich architectural heritage is now a priority. Trinity Lane's stone walls have recently been painstakingly cleaned over a two year period, using traditional methods.

Above: Concealed within dimly lit St. Edward's Passage are cafés, a theatre and bookshops. One of these is The Haunted Bookshop, said to be frequented by the ghost of a long-skirted lady of bygone era. She walks up the stairs and disappears, to be heard rattling crockery somewhere on the first floor.

In St. Edward's Passage is the tiny 13th century church of St. Edward King and Martyr, referred to as 'The Cradle of the Reformation' because early religious reformers preached there.

Left: A stone angel watches over busker and bicycles in Trinity Street.

Opposite: Trinity Lane.

133

Little St. Mary's Lane, with an original gas lamp.

Much of the layout has remained unaltered for a millennium, but significant times have inevitably left their mark. In the early 1300s, a general commercial decline made it simple for the colleges to purchase land and clear areas of the town. Henry VIII's religious politics later played a major part in changing the townscape when he legalised monastic redevelopment and promoted the University's expansion. During the Second World War, Cambridge's beautifully carved stone structures escaped relatively unscathed from bombing, although in Bridge Street, the walls of Whewell's Court bear shrapnel marks from an air attack.

The city's buildings integrate in a pleasing and quirky patchwork of different styles, despite their motley origins. Clues to former ways of life are found in gas lamps, iron railings and stone slabs worn away by the passage of countless feet. In New Square, near Christ's Pieces, outlines of old window shutters can be seen, where soot from many years of domestic coal fires has shadowed the exposed brickwork.

After the town's common fields were privatised, or 'enclosed', in the early 1800s, Cambridge expanded rapidly. Uniformity of design was a strong feature of this housing boom, and gave rise to many attractive rows of cottages. Charles Humfrey, the Kite area's leading builder, used devices such as porticoes, and false windows around New Square to attempt a Classical symmetry. A further spread of larger houses appeared in west Cambridge from around the 1870s, when the colleges finally began to recognise that their fellows could marry.

People have always lived and worked in the city, and much as in previous times, today's residents are a mixture of academics and townsfolk. This gives a homely atmosphere to the bustle in Cambridge that enables it to bear its venerable traditions with an easy charm.

Left: Waiting for the milkman. Domestic life is evident around Cambridge, often close to the small oases of city churchyards such as that of St. Botolph's Church, that has been left to grow wild as a nature haven.

Right: St.Botolph's Lane

Overleaf: New Square

HOBSON'S CONDUIT

Town and Gown successfully united nearly 400 years ago to create Hobson's Conduit, the stream that channels clean spring water into Cambridge town centre from Nine Wells near the Gog Magog Hills.

This skilfully constructed waterway was a remedial necessity, as poor sanitation had aggravated the town's suffering from sporadic epidemics of plague during earlier centuries. The chief health hazard was the King's Ditch, dug as a defensive structure encircling the town, but used as an open sewer. In 1574, the University Vice-Chancellor Dr. Andrew Perne proposed diverting water to flush out the King's Ditch, which he considered would be 'a singular benefite for the healthsomeness both of the Universitie and the Towne.....'.

30 years later, Perne's successor Dr. Stephen Perse joined with local businessmen to implement this plan, funding it by public subscription. A stream was brought to the conduit head on Lensfield Road and distributed via three routes. Water from these channels fed the Fellows' bathing pools at Christ's and Emmanuel and conveniently provided fresh water for Hobson's own stables. The open runnels lining Trumpington Street still exist today, providing a challenge for parking motorists near the Fitzwilliam Museum.

Right: The University's Judge Institute of Management Studies was inaugurated by the Queen in 1996 on the former site of Addenbrooke's Hospital. Hobson's Conduit provided water for the old hospital's laundry next door, which has now become Brown's Restaurant.

Hobson's Conduit

The famous carrier Thomas Hobson was an energetic sponsor of the conduit scheme. Immortalised by the term 'Hobson's Choice, that or none', he refused customers the choice of horse hired out to them. He insisted they took the horse that had rested longest, regardless of its age or temperament. Hobson generously funded the fine Jacobean fountain that was moved from Market Hill after the Great Fire of 1849 to its present location at the conduit head on the corner of Lensfield Road.

THE FITZWILLIAM MUSEUM

The imposing Corinthian façade of the Fitzwilliam Museum announces its presence in grand Classical statement, and within, wonderful galleries of treasures from ancient civilisations live up to this promise.

Known as 'The Fitz', it is a marvellous bonus to culture in Cambridge and one of the best fine art museums in the world. It was endowed in 1816 by the generous bequest of Richard, 7th Viscount Fitzwilliam, an alumnus of Trinity Hall. An avid collector of illuminated manuscripts, books, engravings and paintings (including some by Titian and Rembrandt), he left the handsome sum of £100,000 to build a museum to house his distinguished collection for the benefit of posterity.

The architect of this palatial building, George Basevi, fell to his death from Ely Cathedral in a tragic accident eight years after work began in 1837, and he did not see its completion. Today, the Fitz continues to acquire important works of art and antiquities, while expanding its buildings to accommodate them.

Left: The Fitz lions herald its importance as the museum that held the first national collection of paintings. According to local legend these same lions awake and prowl the streets of Cambridge after midnight, devouring young children who are not in bed.

THE BOTANIC GARDEN

A short walk away from the centre of Cambridge, not far from Coe Fen, is the University Botanic Garden. There the intimate beauty of college gardens is exchanged for a vista of open space dominated by a variety of enormous trees. Many of these are indigenous to other continents and some, such as the giant redwoods, are the oldest specimens of their kind to be found in Britain.

The Botanic Garden's present site is its second home. The original setting was a five acre plot opposite the Museum of Archaeology and Anthropology in Downing Street. This piece of land, together with the buildings of the 'Mansion House', once part of the Austin Friary, were bought in 1760 by Rev. R. Walker. He donated the property to the University and two years later the Public Physic Garden was founded to grow plants for medicinal purposes, most specifically for the use of the University's medical students. 'Conveniently disposed and well-watered', it was modelled on the lines of Chelsea Physic Garden.

In the 1820s, John Stevens Henslow, Cambridge Professor of Botany, focused on the practical scientific study of plants themselves, rather than research into their medical usefulness alone. A co-founder of the Cambridge Philosophical Society and a visionary teacher, Henslow was as at that time influential in shaping the career of Charles Darwin. Henslow was inspired by the adventurous exploration and discovery of plants that was taking place abroad and wished to establish somewhere for the propagation and study of his great love, trees.

It was soon clear that the Garden needed more space than was available in the city centre. In 1831, encouraged by Henslow, the University bought 50 acres of cornfields on the London Road from Trinity Hall.

The gardens provide an ideal habitat for many bird species. Moorhens, coots and ducks frequent the lake and stream, and robins, those perennial English favourites, hop about cheerfully.

Right: The fountains are an attractive focal point within the gardens.

Much hard work followed this purchase. Ambitious planting schemes were carried out under the supervision of the first curator, Andrew Murray. A winding path edged by a belt of trees encircled the garden and creative landscaping within displayed the distinctive attributes of each species to pleasing advantage. An existing old gravel pit was given a new lease of life as the lake. The original layout has remained relatively intact since that time, and a lime tree planted at the formal opening of the new garden on November 2nd, 1846 can still be seen next to the main gate on Trumpington Road.

The plants flourished in their carefully organised beds and glasshouses. By the 1870s, the garden's collection of trees and plants was surpassed only by Kew. A specimen of the plant Anacharis Alsinastrum, or Canadian Water Weed, grew rather too well, however. In 1848, the curator innocently introduced it from a tub in the Botanic Garden into the Conduit stream. From here it travelled to the river, and within four years it had multiplied so prolifically that boats struggled to navigate the river, drainage was difficult, and rowing, swimming and fishing were also impeded.

Hobson's Conduit provides water for irrigation and, sympathetic to its wildlife, the garden shuns the use of artificial fertilisers and pesticides. Relaxed contemplation of the fountains is very likely to be enhanced by a symphony of enthusiastic birdsong.

As a University establishment, the Botanic Garden is of worldwide significance in research across many different disciplines, ranging from archaeology to genetics, as well as botany. The Meteorological Office in Berkshire uses information from the daily weather records that have been maintained there since 1904.

There are over 10,000 varieties of plant and tree species. About a quarter of these may be found in the garden's spectacular glasshouse range, where different worlds of smell, shape, colour, texture and temperature exist. The contrasts provided by the Temperate, Cactus, Alpine or Tropical areas evoke a strong geographic presence, from humid tropical forest to arid desert.

Outside, the variety of habitats has evolved to include a bog garden, winter garden, rock garden, scented garden and stream area, and even a grass maze. Skilful planting allows the different species to be studied interactively within an organised environment, rather than individually. There is an abundance of sensory delight available in the Botanic Garden all year round, for serious botanist and young child alike.

Overleaf: The glasshouses are a special feature of the Botanic Garden, and are well worth a visit in their own right.

GRANTCHESTER

The River Cam continues its lazy meandering habit for the two miles between Silver Street Bridge and the charming village of Grantchester, but reverts to its much older name of Granta, believed to mean 'great'.

A leisurely punt upriver, or a stroll from Newnham across the rural expanse of Grantchester Meadows are favoured forms of gentle exercise. These exertions are rewarded either by afternoon tea at the Orchard or some stronger brew from one of the village's comfortable pubs. Regardless of which quintessential English refreshment is chosen, Grantchester remains a vital part of the Cambridge experience.

Grantchester is very old, and its history has intertwined with that of Cambridge over the centuries. The Romans are believed to have planned the *Via Devana*, their route northwards, to coincide with an existing track that forded the river easily at Grantchester. However, Castle Hill's chalk ridge probably influenced the Roman engineers in favour of siting their fort at Cambridge. It is thought that they then realigned their road to serve the fort there. The remains of a Roman building have been found in Grantchester, but little further excavation has been done.

A Grantchester resident of the 1800s, S.P. Widnall, wrote of a mystery concerning large quantities of red bricks that were regularly ploughed up in a field formerly known as 'Castle Furlong'. A lack of suitable clay pits nearby suggests that these probably came from an ancient structure rather than from a brick kiln. Could a castle once have existed here, as the name suggests?

Rupert Brooke and his talented circle of friends, novelists E.M Forster and Virginia Woolf, philosophers Bertrand Russell and Ludwig Wittgenstein, as well as the outstanding economist Maynard Keynes, spent many carefree happy hours wandering Grantchester Meadows near the Orchard Tea Gardens. The tea gardens have been allowed to grow semi-wild, and remain virtually unchanged to this day.

Left and Far Left: The tea gardens began by chance in 1897 when some Cambridge students requested to have their tea served under the spring blossoms of the orchard apple trees. By the time Rupert lodged there, it was already a favourite haunt with the University crowd. Since the 1930s, it has become a tradition during the celebratory May Week for sleep-deprived students to punt upstream to the Orchard for an outdoor breakfast of champagne and strawberries after dancing the night away at one of the May Balls. Traditional English teas with cake and scones with honey, jam and cream may be enjoyed all year round.

Widnall, an ingenious craftsman, lived at the Old Vicarage in the 1800s. He landscaped the gardens and built a folly, where he held theatre productions and experimented at early photography. Some years after his death, the Old Vicarage became home to the poet Rupert Brooke, who was a Classics scholar at King's in Cambridge.

Shortly before graduating in 1909 Rupert took rooms at Orchard House, seeking a quieter, more reflective life in Grantchester. This proved a vain hope. Admiring females assiduously surrounded the handsome, popular Rupert, who hosted frequent tea and bathing parties for his group of friends, the 'neo-pagans'. Rupert's patient landlady grew tired of his hectic bohemian social life, so he moved to lodgings next door at the Old Vicarage. Here he fell in love with Widnall's beautiful garden, by then romantically overgrown.

The 'Grantchester Grind' is the short walk or cycle from the edge of Cambridge across the meadows to the village. These Grantchester Meadows were bought by King's in 1798: part of a large amount of property the college accumulated within the village over the centuries. King's has helped Grantchester to preserve much of its character.

Overleaf: Wright's Row, a picturesque example of remaining thatched cottages in Grantchester. They were not originally built as a continuous row, as can be seen from the different roof levels.

During a bout of homesickness in Berlin, Rupert wrote his famous poem 'The Old Vicarage, Grantchester', immortalising his sense of time standing still amidst such perfection. The final lines echo this:

> *......oh! Yet*
> *Stands the Church clock at ten to three?*
> *And is there honey still for tea?*

'Ten to three' was artistic licence, as the clock had in fact stopped at a quarter to eight. On the feast day of England's patron saint St. George, the 23rd April 1915, Rupert died while serving during the Great War, only months after writing his deeply patriotic poem 'The Soldier'. He was buried in 'a foreign field that is forever England' under the shade of an olive tree on the Greek island of Skyros. As a mark of respect, Grantchester clock was set at ten to three.

100 years earlier Lord Byron also enjoyed Grantchester's rustic delights, while studying at Trinity. He loved to swim and dive in the secluded pool now known as Byron's Pool. A local tale recounts that many years ago, someone drowned there, and Grantchester denied liability for burial costs, leaving the neighbouring parish of Trumpington to pay for the burial. Later, when the two parishes allegedly disputed the boundary line, close to where the drowning took place, this was recalled and Trumpington was favoured with ownership of a few acres on the Grantchester side of Byron's Pool.

Corpus Christi has strong connections with Grantchester as 'patrons of the parish living' since 1380. The college symbols of pelicans and lilies are seen within the church and churchyard. In 1452 King's bought The Manor House and its farm, which it used as a 'home farm' and also as a refuge for the fellows in times of plague. According to legend, the ancient Manor House had secret passages leading from the cellars to King's College Chapel. Two short collapsed tunnels do exist, but recent opinion is more prosaic, and they are deemed instead to have been rather grand drains.

Right: Early evening at Byron's Pool

THE AMERICAN CEMETERY

On a hillside near Cambridge, an expanse of white marble headstones radiates out in concentric curves towards the horizon. Latin crosses, and Stars of David for those of Jewish faith, mark the graves of 3811 members of the American armed forces who sacrificed their lives in World War II. The visual impact of such a vast quantity of gravestones is emphasised by peaceful fields spread out beyond and below, and underlines the enormity of wartime loss.

The University of Cambridge donated the 30-acre site for America's only World War II cemetery in the British Isles. It was dedicated in 1956 to the men of all the American armed forces who died between 1942 and 1945. East Anglia had a strong United States Air Force presence during the war, and many buried here took part in the air bombardment of North West Europe.

The Memorial has a chapel and a museum with a campaign map engraved by David Kindersley's Cambridge workshop. A line of narrow rectangular pools, bordered by roses, leads to the Memorial. Beside these pools is the long stone Wall of the Missing, carved with the names of a further 5127 American servicemen who 'rest in unknown graves'.

Right and overleaf: The American Cemetery, a place of light and shadow.

St. Catherine's Snowcat

ANDREW PEARCE

On the college Backs at dawn, I feel privileged to take in this tranquil scene. An early mist slowly dissolved by the rising sun, the silence occasionally peppered with the sound of nature - the yaffle of a woodpecker, splash of a jumping fish, and the chatter of a family of long-tailed tits. I have encountered much early morning fauna here over the years: a superb bonus of rising early with the camera. It is this peaceful rural atmosphere of a richly historic city, hosting much natural beauty, that I have sought to portray in this book. For me the attraction remains compelling; for despite countless photographic forays into Cambridge I find the city is always the same, yet different.

KIM WALLIS

Cambridge's beauty is a constant inspiration to me and its story, both past and the unfolding present, is fascinating. The wealth of interesting fact and legend has made it rewarding to write this brief version of its tale. My challenge has been choosing what to include, and what should be abandoned. I owe a great deal to the generous support and comprehensive knowledge of Nick James, who has gently weeded out various inaccuracies, and to the kind assistance of the colleges' archivists and historians. Thank you, Andrew, for your wonderful photographs that have provided the focus for writing this book, and Debi, for your patient help with the editing.

Jesus Green

ACKNOWLEDGEMENTS

Special thanks to Allan Brigham, Barbara Moss, David Johnson, Louise Evans, Janet, Clair Goodhead, Don and the staff at Jessops, Streamline Colour Laboratories, Graeme Down, Steven Pearce, Gail Bradfield, Marie Carden, Nicky Boardman, Jeremy McInerny, Diana Sutcliffe, Anne Moore, Malcolm Safford, Paula Sears, and also Juliette, David, Nina and Anthony for their tolerance and cheerful company.

Thanks for the expertise and advice of: Trevor and Sheila Bounford, Nicholas James, Robert Henderson, Vernon McElroy, Rod at Scudamore's, Andrew Fogg, Tim Milner and Peter Bullock.

Further thanks to the Master, Bursar and Fellows of the following colleges: Peterhouse, Clare, Pembroke, Corpus Christi, Gonville and Caius, Magdalene, King's, Queens', Jesus, Christ's, St. John's, Trinity, Trinity Hall, Emmanuel, Sidney Sussex, Downing. We are also grateful for the valued information obtained from the colleges' websites.

BIBLIOGRAPHY

History of The College of St. John The Evangelist, Cambridge, Baker, T. *[CUP, 1869]* **The Colleges of Cambridge,** Little, B. *[Adams & Dart, 1973]* **Pembroke College Cambridge A Celebration,** Grimstone, A.V. *[Pembroke College, 1997]* **A History of the University of Cambridge Vol.IV 1870-1990,** Brooke, C.N.L. *[CUP, 1993]* **Sidney Sussex College A Short History,** Scott-Giles, C.W. *[Pendragon Press, 1975]* **The Buildings of England Cambridgeshire,** Pevsner, N. *[Penguin Books Ltd, 1970]* **Bedders, Bulldogs & Bedells: A Cambridge Glossary,** Stubbings, F. *[CUP, 1995]* **Hobson's Conduit The Story of a Cambridgeshire chalk stream,** Gray, E.A. *[Bird's Farm Publications, 1977]* **Cambridge The Hidden History,** Taylor, A. *[Tempus Publishing Ltd, 1999]* **Cambridge,** Reeve, F.A. *[B.T. Batsford Ltd, 1976]* **Town and Gown The 700 Years' War in Cambridge,** Parker, R. *[Patrick Stephens, 1983]* **Cambridge A Short History,** Horridge, G.K. & Janaway, J. *[Ammonite Books, 1987]* **Period Piece A Victorian Childhood,** Raverat, G. *[Clear Press Ltd, 2003]* **A History of Grantchester in the County of Cambridge,** Widnall, S.P. *[Published by author, 1875]* **A History of Queens' College, Cambridge 1448-1986,** Twigg, J. *[The Boydell Press, 1987]* **Clare College and The Founding of Clare Hall,** Eden, R. *[The President & Fellows of Clare Hall in the University of Cambridge, 1998]* **Trinity College An Historical Sketch,** Trevelyan, G.M. *[CUP, 1983]* **Trinity Hall,** Crawley, C. *[Printed for the College, Cambridge University Printing House, 1976]* **Hugh Casson's Cambridge,** Casson, H. *[Phaidon Press Ltd, 1992]* **Cambridge University Botanic Garden Visitor Guide,** Parker J.S. *[CUP, 2002]* **West Cambridgeshire,** An Inventory by the Royal Commission on Historical Monuments *[HMSO, 1968]* **Devas & Pearce's Cambridge,** Devas, C. *[Midsummer Publishing, 2001]*

Queen's Road

Peterhouse Deer Park

INDEX

Following page: The University Library (1934) was designed by Sir Giles Gilbert Scott, who also designed the red telephone box.